FARM ANIMALS

GOATS

by Kathryn Clay

raintree

a Capstone company — publishers for children

Raintree is an imprint of Capstone Global Library Limited, a company incorporated in England and Wales having its
registered office at 264 Banbury Road, Oxford, OX2 7DY – Registered company number: 6695582

www.raintree.co.uk
myorders@raintree.co.uk

Edited by Erika L. Shores
Designed by Ashlee Suker
Picture research by Marcie Spence
Production by Eric Manske

ISBN 978 1 4747 1904 9
20 19 18 17 16 15
10 9 8 7 6 5 4 3 2 1

Photo Credits
Alamy: Junior Bildarchiv, 13; Ardea: John Daniels, 5; iStockphoto: BreatheFitness, 21, RonBaily, 15; Shutterstock:
Andrushchenko Dmytro, 19, Anton Balazh, 11, Dmitrijs Bindemanis, cover, 1, Ignite Lab, 17, Mircea Bezergheanu, 7,
Peter Baxter, 9

We would like to thank Gail Saunders-Smith, PhD, and Dr. Celina Johnson for their invaluable help in the preparation
of this book.

Note to Parents and Teachers

This book describes and illustrates goats. The images support early readers in understanding
the text. The repetition of words and phrases helps early readers learn new words. This book
also introduces early readers to subject-specific vocabulary, which is defined in the Glossary
section. Early readers may need assistance to read some words and to use the Table of contents,
Glossary, Read more, Internet sites and Index sections of the book.

Printed and bound in China.

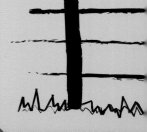

Contents

Meet the goats

A goat's day begins early
on a farm. Farmers milk
goats before the sun rises.

There are about 200 breeds of goat.

Some breeds have long ears.

Others have short ears.

Goats can be black, brown, grey,

red, white or a mix of colours.

Goats are about 1 metre
(3 feet) tall. Most goats weigh
about 54 kilogrammes (120 pounds).

Billies, nannies and kids

Male goats are called billy goats.

Females are nanny goats.

Only female goats make milk.

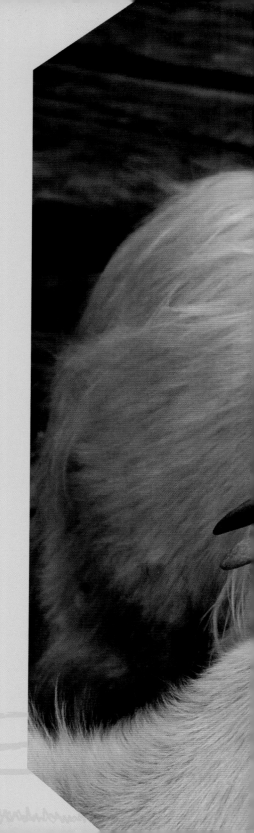

Young goats are called kids.
Between two and four kids are
born at a time. Most goats
live 10 to 12 years.

On the farm

Farmers raise goats for milk and meat. Nanny goats are milked twice a day. Cheese, chocolate and soap are made with goat's milk.

Angora goats are raised
for their thick hair.
The hair is used to make
warm clothing.

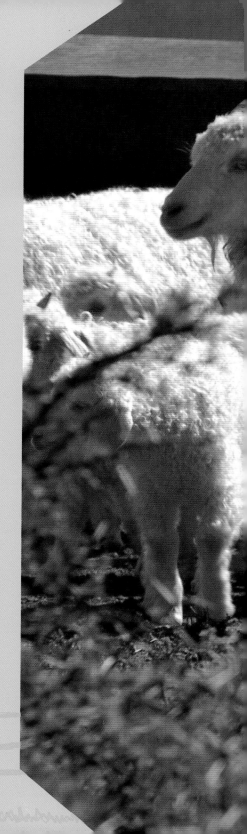

Goat herds rest in pastures when it's warm. They sleep in barns when the weather is cold or rainy.

Playful goats climb on logs.

They swim in ponds.

Goats are at home on the farm.

Glossary

billy goat adult male goat

breed certain kind of animal within an animal group

herd group of goats

kid young goat

nanny goat adult female goat

pasture land where farm animals eat grass and exercise

Read more

Animals on the Farm (Animal All Day!), Joanne Ruelos Diaz (Picture Window Books, 2014)

Farm Animals (World of Farming), Nancy Dickmann (Raintree, 2011)

The Goat in a Coat (Know How to Grow), Karen Clarke (Bear Tails, 2012)

Websites

discoverykids.com/category/animals/
Learn facts about animals and check out photos of all sorts of animals on this website.

kids.nationalgeographic.com/animals
Search for different sorts of animals and learn where they live, what they eat and more.

Index